MW01593268

This book belongs to:

____

Made in the USA
Coppell, TX
20 September 2023

21790985R00065